A Guided Path to Enhance Your Life
through Spiritual Wellness Exercises

The Power of Connection

Growing Through Consistency and Purpose

ANTONIO TYSON

A.D.K.T. Publishing

A.D.K.T. Publishing
Minneapolis, MN

ISBN: 979-8-218-88389-8

Cover and interior design by Jess LaGreca, Mayfly book design

Library of Congress Catalog Number: 2025926107

First Printing: 2026

To all the special people in my life
who had faith and never gave up on me.

Contents

Introduction

"I sought the Lord and He heard, and He answered,
I sought the Lord and He heard, and He answered,
I sought the Lord and He heard and He answered,
That's why I trust Him, that's why I trust Him"
—"Trust in God" (*Elevation Worship, 2023*)

This lyric summarizes why I am creating this interactive journal. I recently recommitted my life to God. I felt a deep joy, but I was also overwhelmed with thoughts about how people would perceive me and what they might think of me now. I asked myself questions like: *How will I stay consistent? How will I stay connected with God? Why now, Lord?*

At the same time, I was pursuing many other goals and felt uncertain about how everything would come together. The only thing I could do was seek the Lord and bring these questions to Him. Over the course of a few weeks, as I continued to seek Him and ask Him to order my steps, things slowly began to fall into place.

Throughout this interactive journal, I will share how God has impacted my life in many ways and reveal the blueprint He has given me to pass on to you. The goal of this journal is to help you stay connected to God. Through this connection, I have discovered my purpose, gained the confidence to face challenges, and found the motivation to pursue the goals God has planted in me.

About Me

My name is Antonio Tyson, and I am an author with a published work. I tear up just thinking about it because becoming a published author has been one of my greatest dreams—a dream of creating, inspiring, and helping others. I never imagined that my first publication would take this form, but I am so grateful that God has led me to share this interactive journal with you.

I have always believed that my life's purpose is to inspire, support, and teach others. Looking back at all the jobs I've held since the age of fourteen, a common thread has always been service. My first job at Arlington Recreation Center in Saint Paul was the beginning of my journey toward teaching and supporting young people.

Fast forward to today, I serve as a school counselor, working primarily with middle school students, though I also have experience with elementary and high school students. Beyond counseling, I've coached a variety of sports, including basketball, flag football, and badminton. I've also served as a basketball referee and recently began refereeing volleyball.

Through all these roles, I can clearly see how God has shaped my path. This interactive journal has given me an even deeper understanding of my purpose and how God continues to call me to serve in different ways.

Purpose of the Journal

One of the biggest challenges I have faced is learning how to stay connected to God each day. With so many distractions, temptations, responsibilities, and unexpected life events, it can be difficult to remain consistently connected. Too often, I leaned on my own understanding of what was happening in my life instead of fully trusting God.

Many times, we tell ourselves that once we return to fellowship or attend church, we will reconnect with God. And in that moment, it may feel true; hearing a message can inspire us and give us the sense that we are back on track spiritually. But the real question is: *Will that connection last?*

Ask yourself: *How did you feel after attending church, receiving the message, jotting down notes, and fellowshipping with others? For me, I felt great, encouraged, inspired, and ready for whatever was to come. I imagine you may have felt the same way. But then the real question is: How long did that feeling last?*

What challenges did you face during the week that followed? Were you able to overcome those challenges? Were you able to apply what you had learned and go back to the notes you had written down from that message?

These were the very questions I had to ask myself as I began my journey back to salvation and a deeper relationship with God. It was during this time that I realized I needed help. I had to seek Him for direction on how to stay connected, especially with everything I knew was about to unfold in my life.

As a school counselor, the beginning of the school year always brings a whirlwind of responsibilities—and to be honest, it can be quite stressful. On top of that, I'm learning a new sport to officiate, launching a business, preparing to start school in October to pursue two additional licenses, and working toward a few more certifications in training and coaching.

All of this was happening while I continued the deeper work of transforming my life back into alignment with how God intended it to be. I realized the only one I could truly rely on was God. I needed His help and support, because if I allowed overthinking and stress to take control, I knew it would threaten my connection with Him. *I prayed and asked God: "Lord, what can*

I do to stay connected to You each day? Please show me how I can apply Your Word to my life daily so that I may live in dominion and claim victory over the challenges I face."

The Lord answered my prayer and provided me with a blueprint for staying connected to Him each day. I am so grateful that He responded because through this I have experienced tremendous spiritual and personal growth. Even more, I am now living my purpose. I know that I have authority over my life, because I am led by Him.

I want you to experience the same transformation that I have experienced, and that is the purpose behind creating and sharing this interactive journal. Throughout this journal, I will provide insight, tools, motivation, and activities to guide you at every step of the way.

I want you to realize that you have dominion over your life and the power to overcome the challenges you face. Two essential components of this journey are understanding your daily habits and applying God's Word to your life. Daily habits matter because they can be either positive or negative, shaping each day and ultimately influencing the direction your life takes.

Additionally, being disconnected from God can create a space where we lose touch with reality and become blind to what is happening around us. Staying connected to God, however, opens a clear path, allowing us to see and live out the vision and purpose He has for our lives.

I invite you to take this **ninety-day journey** with me. Together, we will unlock your potential, strengthen your faith, and claim the victories God has already prepared for you.

Spiritual Wellness Exercises (SWE)

The **Spiritual Wellness Exercises (SWE)** have been life-changing for me. They've helped me grow in my faith, stay consistent, and overcome life's challenges. I practice them daily to connect with God and apply His Word.

In this journal, I'll share how God first revealed the SWE to me, how I've used them in my own journey, and how you can apply them for growth and guidance.

What are SWE?

They are daily practices designed to align your mind, body, spirit, and soul with God's Word:

1. **Morning Check-in:** Bible verse and prayer.
2. **Mind:** Restore and grounding.
3. **Body:** Wellness activity & mindful food intake.
4. **Spirit & Soul:** Applying God's Word with an action plan.
5. **Reflection & Prayer:** Evening review and prayer.

Each one has been essential in keeping me rooted in God's presence, and throughout this journal, I'll show you how they've transformed my walk with Him.

To support the SWE, this journal also includes:

- **Renewing the Mind Principles/Thoughts.** For focus, clarity, and capacity-building.
- **Motivation & Inspiration.** To keep you motivated in your walk with Christ.
- **Prayers.** Personal prayers I use daily. You can pray to them as written or use them as a guide to create your own.

Day 1—Your Breakthrough Begins

oday marks the start of your breakthrough. We're building daily habits through the **Spiritual Wellness Exercises (SWE)**—practices that will keep you connected to God and set a foundation for growth. I'll guide you through Day 1 with examples from my own journey, and I'll be right here cheering you on as you create habits that lead to success in every area of your life.

STEP 1: ACKNOWLEDGE YOUR FEELINGS

Before we begin, pause and reflect on how you're feeling right now. Write it down:

I feel _____ .

I feel _____ .

Then, dig deeper:

I feel _____ because _____

_____ .

I feel _____ because _____

_____ .

When I started, I felt **overwhelmed** because I didn't believe I had the time for such a big commitment. I also felt **angry**, reflecting on past decisions I regretted before giving my life back to Christ.

STEP 2: TURN FEELINGS INTO PRAYER

Now, use those feelings from above to create a prayer. Here's mine from when I began:

"Lord, I come to You feeling overwhelmed and angry. I fear I won't have enough time for all I need to do, and I'm burdened by past mistakes. Please show me how to stay committed to You and release the anger holding me back."

Write your prayer below:

STEP 3: DAILY MORNING CHECK-IN (BIBLE VERSE)

Choose a verse that speaks to you. This will be today's check-in with God. One that shaped me is **Matthew 7:7–8**.

When reading a verse, ask:

1. Why is God sharing this with me?
2. What stands out?
3. How can I apply this today?

STEP 4: SPIRIT & SOUL. ACTION PLAN

Scripture often stirs both spirit and soul—it gives us direction and inspires action. Create a simple action plan for today by connecting God's Word to your goals.

Example Action Plan

- Release anger
- Maximize my time
- Seize opportunities today
- Finish student schedules

At night, reflect. Celebrate what you accomplished and note where you can grow.

My Reflection on Matthew 7:7–8
　　Here's what I've learned:

1. God asks us to connect with Him—through our voice, eyes, and actions—so we don't carry life's burdens alone.
2. I noticed my anger and being overwhelmed were rising from past choices and current responsibilities.
3. To release anger, I accepted God's forgiveness and took ownership of my decisions. To manage being overwhelmed, God led me to delete social media. It was tough, but it freed up time to seize new opportunities—and I've accomplished so much since.

DAILY MORNING CHECK-IN. BIBLE VERSE(S)

Starting your day this way opens the door for God to speak, guide, and reveal His plan—sometimes immediately, sometimes later. The key is connection and application.

What will your Bible verse be? _____

_____

_____

_____

Why do you think God shared this verse/message? _____

_____

_____

_____

What stands out to you? _____

_____

_____

_____

How can you apply this to your life today? _____

_____

_____

_____

SPIRIT & SOUL. ACTION PLAN

(Write 3–5 simple goals for the day that align with God's Word.)

1.

2.

3.

4.

5.

You've just completed one of the **Spiritual Wellness Exercises (SWE)**. Starting your day this way prepares you with the armor of Christ.

MIND: RESTORE & GROUNDING

This step is about renewing your mind and staying grounded in Christ. Our thoughts often limit us, but renewing your mind daily unlocks your potential. For me, I use my commute to listen to an inspirational song, sermon, or podcast that restores and grounds me.

Examples I've used:

- Song: *"He Saw the Best in Me"*—Marvin Sapp
- Sermon: *"Renewing Your Mind God's Way"*—Creflo Dollar

When I practice this SWE, I ask myself:

1. How did I feel afterward?
2. What did I learn, and how can I apply it today?

Your Turn: How will you renew your mind today?

Song: _____

Sermon: _____

Podcast: _____

Reflections:

How do you feel now? _____

BODY

Caring for your body strengthens you physically, mentally, and spiritually. This isn't about strict diets or long workouts—it's about small, intentional choices each day. For me, writing down my wellness plan helps me stay accountable. Sometimes I even combine this SWE with others—for example, cycling while listening to a sermon or inspirational music.

Wellness Activity	Food Intake

Reflection & Prayer

REFLECTION & PRAYER (END OF DAY)

At night, reflect on your day and close with prayer. You can repeat the prayer you wrote earlier, expand it, or write a new one based on the day's events.

Prompts to guide your reflection:

- I enjoyed this SWE because . . .
- I felt connected to God when . . .
- Today was . . .
- I feel blessed because . . .
- What stood out most about my day was . . .

Reflection helps you grow and see how God is moving in your life daily.

AUTHOR EXAMPLE #1

(Use this content on the next page to create Example #1.)

SPIRITUAL WELLNESS EXERCISE (SWE)

Bible Verse: 2 Samuel 22:7

What stands out to you?

God shared this message with me as He knew entering Speak the Word Church after Twenty-two years would be very emotional for me.

How can you apply this to your life today?

I called out to the Lord to provide me with guidance as shame was something that prevented me from staying connected with God. I failed many times before but knowing that the Lord hears you and that I am forgiven is how I have been able to stay connected. I apply this to my life especially if I am feeling a negative emotion. I know that I can rely and ask Him for help to guide me through and ensure that I stay on the right path.

Spirit & Soul. Action Plan

- Pray to release the shame.
- Share with someone that I recommitted my life back to Christ.
- Go on a walk and reflect on the experience I had today entering the church building.

Mind. Restore & Grounding

- Sermon. "Daily Habits for Conquering Life's Challenges Part 2 " (Randy Morrison).
- In watching this sermon, the thing that stood out the most to me and was an aha moment was thinking about my daily habits. I knew that in order for my change to happen and stay connect with God, I had to think and begin to change some of my daily habits.

Wellness Activity

I will walk for thirty minutes, reflect on my experience, and think of my prayer. I am going to talk with God about the shame I felt for so long.

Food Intake

Today, I will have coffee, a bagel with cream cheese. I will have a sandwich from Erberts and Gerberts—most likely the Flash sandwich.

Reflection & Prayer

Today was very surreal feeling, going back to church. I was very inspired to see the pastor still filled with a lot of joy, that is one of the first things that stood out the most to me as I was reflecting on my feelings while standing for praise and worship. Thank you, Lord, for giving me the ability to have faith and have a new process through you. I don't have fear of the unknown, I am confident, and my approach is through faith, accepting all challenges that come my way. Through faith I will win and I claim the victory, Lord.

Spiritual Wellness Exercises:
Days 2–10

SPIRITUAL WELLNESS EXERCISE (SWE): DAY 2

Date: _____

Bible Verse:

What stands out to you?	Spirit & Soul. Action Plan
How can you apply this to your life today?	Mind. Restore & Grounding

Wellness Activity	Food Intake

Reflection & Prayer

SPIRITUAL WELLNESS EXERCISE (SWE): DAY 3

Date: _____

Bible Verse:

What stands out to you?

Spirit & Soul. Action Plan

How can you apply this
to your life today?

Mind. Restore & Grounding

Wellness Activity

Food Intake

Reflection & Prayer

SPIRITUAL WELLNESS EXERCISE (SWE): DAY 4

Date: _____

Bible Verse:

What stands out to you?	Spirit & Soul. Action Plan
How can you apply this to your life today?	Mind. Restore & Grounding

Wellness Activity	Food Intake

Reflection & Prayer

SPIRITUAL WELLNESS EXERCISE (SWE): DAY 5

Date: _____

Bible Verse:

What stands out to you?	Spirit & Soul. Action Plan
How can you apply this to your life today?	Mind. Restore & Grounding

Wellness Activity	Food Intake

Reflection & Prayer

SPIRITUAL WELLNESS EXERCISE (SWE): DAY 6

Date: _____

Bible Verse:

What stands out to you?	Spirit & Soul. Action Plan
How can you apply this to your life today?	Mind. Restore & Grounding

Wellness Activity	Food Intake

Reflection & Prayer

SPIRITUAL WELLNESS EXERCISE (SWE): DAY 7

Date: _____

Bible Verse:

What stands out to you?	Spirit & Soul. Action Plan
How can you apply this to your life today?	Mind. Restore & Grounding

Wellness Activity	Food Intake

Reflection & Prayer

SPIRITUAL WELLNESS EXERCISE (SWE): DAY 8

Date: _____

Bible Verse:

What stands out to you?

Spirit & Soul. Action Plan

How can you apply this
to your life today?

Mind. Restore & Grounding

Wellness Activity

Food Intake

Reflection & Prayer

SPIRITUAL WELLNESS EXERCISE (SWE): DAY 9

Date: _____

Bible Verse:

What stands out to you?	Spirit & Soul. Action Plan
How can you apply this to your life today?	Mind. Restore & Grounding

Wellness Activity	Food Intake

Reflection & Prayer

SPIRITUAL WELLNESS EXERCISE (SWE): DAY 10

Date: _____

Bible Verse:

What stands out to you?

Spirit & Soul. Action Plan

How can you apply this
to your life today?

Mind. Restore & Grounding

Wellness Activity

Food Intake

Reflection & Prayer

MOTIVATIONAL MESSAGE #1

Focus on the process as your breakthrough is on the way.

Spiritual Wellness Exercises:
Days 11–22

SPIRITUAL WELLNESS EXERCISE (SWE): DAY 11

Date: _____

Bible Verse:

What stands out to you?

Spirit & Soul. Action Plan

How can you apply this
to your life today?

Mind. Restore & Grounding

Wellness Activity

Food Intake

Reflection & Prayer

SPIRITUAL WELLNESS EXERCISE (SWE): DAY 12

Date: _____

Bible Verse:

What stands out to you?	**Spirit & Soul. Action Plan**
How can you apply this to your life today?	**Mind. Restore & Grounding**

Wellness Activity	Food Intake

Reflection & Prayer

SPIRITUAL WELLNESS EXERCISE (SWE): DAY 13

Date: _____

Bible Verse:

What stands out to you?

Spirit & Soul. Action Plan

How can you apply this
to your life today?

Mind. Restore & Grounding

Wellness Activity

Food Intake

Reflection & Prayer

SPIRITUAL WELLNESS EXERCISE (SWE): DAY 14

Date: _____

Bible Verse:

What stands out to you?	Spirit & Soul. Action Plan
How can you apply this to your life today?	Mind. Restore & Grounding

Wellness Activity	Food Intake

Reflection & Prayer

SPIRITUAL WELLNESS EXERCISE (SWE): DAY 15

Date: _____

Bible Verse:

| What stands out to you?

How can you apply this to your life today? | **Spirit & Soul. Action Plan**

Mind. Restore & Grounding |

| Wellness Activity | Food Intake |

Reflection & Prayer

SPIRITUAL WELLNESS EXERCISE (SWE): DAY 16

Date: _____

Bible Verse:

What stands out to you?	Spirit & Soul. Action Plan
How can you apply this to your life today?	Mind. Restore & Grounding

Wellness Activity	Food Intake

Reflection & Prayer

SPIRITUAL WELLNESS EXERCISE (SWE): DAY 17

Date: _____

Bible Verse:

What stands out to you?	Spirit & Soul. Action Plan
How can you apply this to your life today?	Mind. Restore & Grounding

Wellness Activity	Food Intake

Reflection & Prayer

SPIRITUAL WELLNESS EXERCISE (SWE): DAY 18

Date: _____

Bible Verse:

What stands out to you?	Spirit & Soul. Action Plan
How can you apply this to your life today?	Mind. Restore & Grounding

Wellness Activity	Food Intake

Reflection & Prayer

SPIRITUAL WELLNESS EXERCISE (SWE): DAY 19

Date: _____

Bible Verse:

What stands out to you?	Spirit & Soul. Action Plan
How can you apply this to your life today?	Mind. Restore & Grounding

Wellness Activity	Food Intake

Reflection & Prayer

SPIRITUAL WELLNESS EXERCISE (SWE): DAY 20

Date: _____

Bible Verse:

What stands out to you?	Spirit & Soul. Action Plan
How can you apply this to your life today?	Mind. Restore & Grounding

Wellness Activity	Food Intake

Reflection & Prayer

SPIRITUAL WELLNESS EXERCISE (SWE): DAY 21

Date: _____

Bible Verse:

What stands out to you?	Spirit & Soul. Action Plan
How can you apply this to your life today?	Mind. Restore & Grounding

Wellness Activity	Food Intake

Reflection & Prayer

SPIRITUAL WELLNESS EXERCISE (SWE): DAY 22

Date: _____

Bible Verse:

What stands out to you? How can you apply this to your life today?	Spirit & Soul. Action Plan Mind. Restore & Grounding

Wellness Activity	Food Intake

Reflection & Prayer

MOTIVATIONAL MESSAGE #2

Stay consistent to unlock your potential.

REFLECTION & CHECK-IN

Congratulations, you've completed twenty-two days! Take time to reflect on your journey so far. Review your nightly reflections and consider how the Spiritual Wellness Exercises (SWE) have impacted your life. You may want to highlight a specific day, prayer, or message that stood out.

Reflection Prompts:

- What challenge have you overcome?
- How has SWE influenced your relationships (family, friends, work)?
- What new things are you discovering about yourself?
- Have others noticed a change in you?

Example:

One of the biggest challenges I faced was worrying about how people would see me in Christ. I thought they would only remember who I used to be and wouldn't accept the changes I was making. That fear of judgment could have kept me from living my truth and staying connected to God.

Journaling helped me reflect on moments when I could share my faith naturally. For instance, a colleague noticed I seemed low and asked how I was doing. I realized I had been worrying about things out of my control—things that often create a disconnect with God. Worry can take over your mind and actions, and I know from experience how it can affect your entire day.

I'm grateful my colleague checked in because it reminded me to renew my mind. Once I did, I felt restored and confident, remembering who I am in Christ. That shift gave me the courage to share my journey, and soon other colleagues began opening up about their struggles, saying they felt disconnected from God. I promised them that once I finished this journal, I would share it and invite them to use it too.

My hope is that this journal becomes a tool for you to connect with God and with others. Some parts of your journey might feel deeply personal, and that's okay. You don't have to share everything. But there's something powerful about telling your story—about seeing how God is moving in your life and in the lives of those around you. My prayer is that as you reflect and share, we can create a community of encouragement, growth, and fellowship, celebrating how God is transforming us every day.

Use this space to reflect on your own growth:

RENEWING THE MIND

During this phase, we'll add "**Renewing the Mind Principles/Thoughts.**"

Example Principle: "Have an Attitude of Acceptance"

What does this mean to you? _____

_____

_____

How could you apply it in your life? _____

_____

_____

Example (from my journey):

Each day, I renew my mind by maintaining an attitude ready to accept the challenges God places before me. I choose not to get frustrated or upset when someone comes to me with an issue. Instead, I see it as an opportunity for growth and a chance to follow God's guidance in handling the situation.

For example, at work, I used to get annoyed when colleagues brought problems my way. My first thought would often be, *This isn't my job*, or *I don't get paid enough for this*. But reframing these moments with an "Attitude of Acceptance" allowed me to see them differently. I realized that my approach could create favor, understanding, and opportunities for future growth.

By keeping this mindset throughout the week, I noticed new opportunities at work, gained more freedom in my role, and strengthened my relationships with colleagues. Approaching challenges with acceptance opened doors I hadn't imagined.

As you go through this journal, you will encounter more "Renewing of the Mind Thoughts." I encourage you to consider applying one each week to see how it impacts your thinking and actions. Throughout Days 23–46, you'll see different *"Renewing the Mind Principles"* (examples: patience, commitment, looking forward). Use them to guide your reflection and strengthen your spiritual focus.

AUTHOR EXAMPLE #2

(Use this content on the next page to create Example #2.)

SPIRITUAL WELLNESS EXERCISE (SWE)

Bible Verse: Ephesians 3:12

What stands out to you?

I think He shared this message to remind us that through Him; we should have confidence. The faith that we have in Him is our access point.

How can you apply this to your life today?

What do we have access to? The way that I am going to apply the Word is that I have direct access to Him. The access opens opportunities for me to grow in all areas of my life, and I should be confident in knowing that. Today, I am going to walk around confidently, knowing that I have a direct access point through my faith.

Spirit & Soul. Action Plan

- I am going to stay confident today with tasks at work.
- I am going to make sure that I work in excellence.
- I am going to be more patient with others today.

Mind. Restore & Grounding

"Promises" (Maverick City Music & Naomie Raine) I felt so good after listening to this song; it was exactly what I needed, especially after a long day of work. It made the ride home very enjoyable.

Wellness Activity

I played basketball with a group of friends and did some activation/ mobility exercises.

Food Intake

- Coffee, bagel w/cream cheese
- Cesar salad
- Yogurt
- Protein shake

Reflection & Prayer

Today, I felt so productive, but it was such a long day. I enjoyed playing basketball today with friends as it was a good release and an enjoyable time, even though I didn't shoot the best. Thank You Lord for keeping me confident today as I was getting all my tasks done. I look forward to the next day to stay confident and productive. I pray for my family and friends, that You continue to watch over them and protect them. Amen.

Spiritual Wellness Exercises: Days 23–30

SPIRITUAL WELLNESS EXERCISE (SWE): DAY 23

Date: _____

Bible Verse:

What stands out to you?

How can you apply this
to your life today?

Spirit & Soul. Action Plan

Mind. Restore & Grounding

Wellness Activity

Food Intake

Reflection & Prayer

SPIRITUAL WELLNESS EXERCISE (SWE): DAY 24

Date: _____

Bible Verse:

What stands out to you?	Spirit & Soul. Action Plan
How can you apply this to your life today?	Mind. Restore & Grounding

Wellness Activity	Food Intake

Reflection & Prayer

SPIRITUAL WELLNESS EXERCISE (SWE): DAY 25

Date: _____

Bible Verse:

What stands out to you?	Spirit & Soul. Action Plan
How can you apply this to your life today?	Mind. Restore & Grounding

Wellness Activity	Food Intake

Reflection & Prayer

SPIRITUAL WELLNESS EXERCISE (SWE): DAY 26

Date: _____

Bible Verse:

What stands out to you?	Spirit & Soul. Action Plan
How can you apply this to your life today?	Mind. Restore & Grounding

Wellness Activity	Food Intake

Reflection & Prayer

SPIRITUAL WELLNESS EXERCISE (SWE): DAY 27

Date: _____

Bible Verse:

What stands out to you? How can you apply this to your life today?	Spirit & Soul. Action Plan Mind. Restore & Grounding

Wellness Activity	Food Intake

Reflection & Prayer

SPIRITUAL WELLNESS EXERCISE (SWE): DAY 28

Date: _____

Bible Verse:

What stands out to you?	Spirit & Soul. Action Plan
How can you apply this to your life today?	Mind. Restore & Grounding

Wellness Activity	Food Intake

Reflection & Prayer

SPIRITUAL WELLNESS EXERCISE (SWE): DAY 29

Date: _____

Bible Verse:

What stands out to you?	Spirit & Soul. Action Plan
How can you apply this to your life today?	Mind. Restore & Grounding

Wellness Activity	Food Intake

Reflection & Prayer

SPIRITUAL WELLNESS EXERCISE (SWE): DAY 30

Date: _____

Bible Verse:

What stands out to you?	Spirit & Soul. Action Plan
How can you apply this to your life today?	Mind. Restore & Grounding

Wellness Activity	Food Intake

Reflection & Prayer

RENEWING THE MIND PRINCIPLE/THOUGHT #1

"Rest your mind, for your time and season will come with patience."

We often rush the process of achieving our goals, overlooking the steps and factors needed for completion. I had to ask God to help me overcome my impatience because I could see the finished product and wanted to be at the finish line already. Impatience can bring self-doubt and loss of motivation. This principle reminds us to rest our minds, slow down, and trust God's timing. Recognizing that our timing is not always God's timing helps us stay patient, motivated, and confident as we take each step toward our season.

Spiritual Wellness Exercises:
Days 31–38

SPIRITUAL WELLNESS EXERCISE (SWE): DAY 31

Date: _____

Bible Verse:

What stands out to you?

Spirit & Soul. Action Plan

How can you apply this
to your life today?

Mind. Restore & Grounding

Wellness Activity

Food Intake

Reflection & Prayer

SPIRITUAL WELLNESS EXERCISE (SWE): DAY 32

Date: _____

Bible Verse:

What stands out to you?	Spirit & Soul. Action Plan
How can you apply this to your life today?	Mind. Restore & Grounding

Wellness Activity	Food Intake

Reflection & Prayer

SPIRITUAL WELLNESS EXERCISE (SWE): DAY 33

Date: _____

Bible Verse:

What stands out to you?	Spirit & Soul. Action Plan
How can you apply this to your life today?	Mind. Restore & Grounding

Wellness Activity	Food Intake

Reflection & Prayer

SPIRITUAL WELLNESS EXERCISE (SWE): DAY 34

Date: _____

Bible Verse:

What stands out to you?	Spirit & Soul. Action Plan
How can you apply this to your life today?	Mind. Restore & Grounding

Wellness Activity	Food Intake

Reflection & Prayer

SPIRITUAL WELLNESS EXERCISE (SWE): DAY 35

Date: _____

Bible Verse:

What stands out to you?

Spirit & Soul. Action Plan

How can you apply this
to your life today?

Mind. Restore & Grounding

Wellness Activity

Food Intake

Reflection & Prayer

SPIRITUAL WELLNESS EXERCISE (SWE): DAY 36

Date: _____

Bible Verse:

What stands out to you?	Spirit & Soul. Action Plan
How can you apply this to your life today?	Mind. Restore & Grounding

Wellness Activity	Food Intake

Reflection & Prayer

SPIRITUAL WELLNESS EXERCISE (SWE): DAY 37

Date: _____

Bible Verse:

What stands out to you?	Spirit & Soul. Action Plan
How can you apply this to your life today?	Mind. Restore & Grounding

Wellness Activity	Food Intake

Reflection & Prayer

SPIRITUAL WELLNESS EXERCISE (SWE): DAY 38

Date: _____

Bible Verse:

What stands out to you?	Spirit & Soul. Action Plan
How can you apply this to your life today?	Mind. Restore & Grounding

Wellness Activity	Food Intake

Reflection & Prayer

RENEWING THE MIND PRINCIPLE/THOUGHT #2

"Commitment to the work God has put in front of you to fulfill your purpose."

Commitment is challenging, especially when we don't fully understand our purpose. Sometimes we commit to things outside of God's plan, which can cost us friendships, relationships, and peace. Ask God, *"What do you want me to be committed to?"* to ensure your efforts align with His purpose. For example, as a school counselor, I commit to supporting students and learning from every interaction. This daily commitment prepares me to fulfill my ultimate purpose, which is to serve as a youth pastor one day.

Spiritual Wellness Exercises:
Days 39–46

SPIRITUAL WELLNESS EXERCISE (SWE): DAY 39

Date: _____

> **Bible Verse:**

What stands out to you?	Spirit & Soul. Action Plan
How can you apply this to your life today?	Mind. Restore & Grounding

Wellness Activity	Food Intake

Reflection & Prayer

SPIRITUAL WELLNESS EXERCISE (SWE): DAY 40

Date: _____

Bible Verse:

| What stands out to you?

How can you apply this to your life today? | Spirit & Soul. Action Plan

Mind. Restore & Grounding |

| Wellness Activity | Food Intake |

| Reflection & Prayer |

SPIRITUAL WELLNESS EXERCISE (SWE): DAY 41

Date: _____

Bible Verse:

What stands out to you?	Spirit & Soul. Action Plan
How can you apply this to your life today?	Mind. Restore & Grounding

Wellness Activity	Food Intake

Reflection & Prayer

SPIRITUAL WELLNESS EXERCISE (SWE): DAY 42

Date: _____

Bible Verse:

What stands out to you?	Spirit & Soul. Action Plan
How can you apply this to your life today?	Mind. Restore & Grounding

Wellness Activity	Food Intake

Reflection & Prayer

SPIRITUAL WELLNESS EXERCISE (SWE): DAY 43

Date: _____

Bible Verse:

What stands out to you?	Spirit & Soul. Action Plan
How can you apply this to your life today?	Mind. Restore & Grounding

Wellness Activity	Food Intake

Reflection & Prayer

SPIRITUAL WELLNESS EXERCISE (SWE): DAY 44

Date: _____

Bible Verse:

What stands out to you?	**Spirit & Soul. Action Plan**
How can you apply this to your life today?	**Mind. Restore & Grounding**

Wellness Activity	Food Intake

Reflection & Prayer

SPIRITUAL WELLNESS EXERCISE (SWE): DAY 45

Date: _____

Bible Verse:

What stands out to you?	Spirit & Soul. Action Plan
How can you apply this to your life today?	Mind. Restore & Grounding

Wellness Activity	Food Intake

Reflection & Prayer

SPIRITUAL WELLNESS EXERCISE (SWE): DAY 46

Date: _____

Bible Verse:

What stands out to you?	**Spirit & Soul. Action Plan**
How can you apply this to your life today?	**Mind. Restore & Grounding**

Wellness Activity	Food Intake

Reflection & Prayer

RENEWING THE MIND PRINCIPLE/THOUGHT #3
"Look forward and take action to activate the prayers you have asked for."

Having a forward-looking mindset means embracing the day, including its challenges and opportunities. Often, we dread difficult interactions, which limits our growth and engagement. By changing our perspective, we can approach each situation with readiness and purpose. Taking action with this mindset allows the prayers we've been asking for to begin manifesting as we actively participate in the opportunities God places before us.

BODY RENEWAL

Congratulations on completing forty-six days! Today, take a moment to reflect on your **physical and mental health**. When was the last time you had a check-up, physical, or blood work to check your vitamin and mineral levels? Staying on top of your health is essential—how can we be our best selves if we aren't physically and mentally well? God calls us to strive in all areas of life, and neglecting our health can affect our confidence, mindset, and perception of others.

This is why we track **wellness activities and food intake**. Reflect on how consistent you have been with your wellness routine and the types of foods you've been consuming. Pick a day below and reflect on it—consider how it impacted you and how it might guide your choices for the future.

Pick a Day to Share:

Day _____

Wellness Activity	Food Intake

Reflect on Your Wellness Activity

Today, my wellness activity was: _____

I felt _____ because _____

Reflecting on how you felt and why can help you continue positive habits. If the activity left you feeling negative, explore why and consider how to adjust. For example, I don't usually enjoy cycling uphill, but my friends do. Initially, I felt frustrated, doubted myself, and worried about being judged. These thoughts affected my enjoyment.

To overcome this, I renewed my mind with **an attitude of acceptance**, practiced on smaller hills to build confidence, and focused on my breathing. Eventually, I rode up a steep hill near my house—one I had always walked before. During the ride, I felt God cheering me on and experienced a deep sense of accomplishment.

Reflect on Food Enjoyed

Next, write about a meal or food you truly enjoyed in the past forty-six days. Describe why it was meaningful. For example, one of my favorite desserts is cheesecake from Key's Cafe. I enjoy it because it's fulfilling, delicious, and shared with friends or colleagues, making the experience memorable.

Something I enjoyed eating in the last forty-six days was: _____

Being mindful of what we eat supports our energy, wellness, and ability to fulfill God's purpose for our lives. Consistent reflection helps us understand the impact of our choices and maintain balance in body, mind, and spirit.

Spiritual Wellness Exercises:
Days 47–60

SPIRITUAL WELLNESS EXERCISE (SWE): DAY 47

Date: _____

Bible Verse:

What stands out to you? How can you apply this to your life today?	Spirit & Soul. Action Plan Mind. Restore & Grounding

Wellness Activity	Food Intake

Reflection & Prayer

SPIRITUAL WELLNESS EXERCISE (SWE): DAY 48

Date: _____

Bible Verse:

What stands out to you? How can you apply this to your life today?	Spirit & Soul. Action Plan Mind. Restore & Grounding

Wellness Activity	Food Intake

Reflection & Prayer

SPIRITUAL WELLNESS EXERCISE (SWE): DAY 49

Date: _____

Bible Verse:

What stands out to you?	Spirit & Soul. Action Plan
How can you apply this to your life today?	Mind. Restore & Grounding

Wellness Activity	Food Intake

Reflection & Prayer

SPIRITUAL WELLNESS EXERCISE (SWE): DAY 50

Date: _____

Bible Verse:

What stands out to you? How can you apply this to your life today?	Spirit & Soul. Action Plan Mind. Restore & Grounding

Wellness Activity	Food Intake

Reflection & Prayer

SPIRITUAL WELLNESS EXERCISE (SWE): DAY 51

Date: _____

Bible Verse:

What stands out to you?	Spirit & Soul. Action Plan
How can you apply this to your life today?	Mind. Restore & Grounding

Wellness Activity	Food Intake

Reflection & Prayer

SPIRITUAL WELLNESS EXERCISE (SWE): DAY 52

Date: _____

Bible Verse:

What stands out to you?	**Spirit & Soul. Action Plan**
How can you apply this to your life today?	**Mind. Restore & Grounding**

Wellness Activity	Food Intake

Reflection & Prayer

SPIRITUAL WELLNESS EXERCISE (SWE): DAY 53

Date: _____

Bible Verse:

What stands out to you?

Spirit & Soul. Action Plan

How can you apply this
to your life today?

Mind. Restore & Grounding

Wellness Activity

Food Intake

Reflection & Prayer

SPIRITUAL WELLNESS EXERCISE (SWE): DAY 54

Date: _____

Bible Verse:

What stands out to you?	**Spirit & Soul. Action Plan**
How can you apply this to your life today?	**Mind. Restore & Grounding**

Wellness Activity	Food Intake

Reflection & Prayer

SPIRITUAL WELLNESS EXERCISE (SWE): DAY 55

Date: _____

Bible Verse:

What stands out to you?	Spirit & Soul. Action Plan
How can you apply this to your life today?	Mind. Restore & Grounding

Wellness Activity	Food Intake

Reflection & Prayer

SPIRITUAL WELLNESS EXERCISE (SWE): DAY 56

Date: _____

Bible Verse:

What stands out to you?	Spirit & Soul. Action Plan
How can you apply this to your life today?	Mind. Restore & Grounding

Wellness Activity	Food Intake

Reflection & Prayer

SPIRITUAL WELLNESS EXERCISE (SWE): DAY 57

Date: _____

Bible Verse:

What stands out to you?	Spirit & Soul. Action Plan
How can you apply this to your life today?	Mind. Restore & Grounding

Wellness Activity	Food Intake

Reflection & Prayer

SPIRITUAL WELLNESS EXERCISE (SWE): DAY 58

Date: _____

Bible Verse:

What stands out to you? How can you apply this to your life today?	Spirit & Soul. Action Plan Mind. Restore & Grounding

Wellness Activity	Food Intake

Reflection & Prayer

SPIRITUAL WELLNESS EXERCISE (SWE): DAY 59

Date: _____

Bible Verse:

What stands out to you? How can you apply this to your life today?	Spirit & Soul. Action Plan Mind. Restore & Grounding

Wellness Activity	Food Intake

Reflection & Prayer

SPIRITUAL WELLNESS EXERCISE (SWE): DAY 60

Date: _____

Bible Verse:

What stands out to you?	Spirit & Soul. Action Plan
How can you apply this to your life today?	Mind. Restore & Grounding

Wellness Activity	Food Intake

Reflection & Prayer

MOTIVATIONAL MESSAGE #3

Connection provides clarity.

Spiritual Wellness Exercises:
Days 61–70

SPIRITUAL WELLNESS EXERCISE (SWE): DAY 61

Date: _____

> **Bible Verse:**

What stands out to you?	**Spirit & Soul. Action Plan**
How can you apply this to your life today?	**Mind. Restore & Grounding**

Wellness Activity	Food Intake

Reflection & Prayer

SPIRITUAL WELLNESS EXERCISE (SWE): DAY 62

Date: _____

Bible Verse:

| What stands out to you?

How can you apply this
to your life today? | Spirit & Soul. Action Plan

Mind. Restore & Grounding |

| Wellness Activity | Food Intake |

Reflection & Prayer

97

SPIRITUAL WELLNESS EXERCISE (SWE): DAY 63

Date: _____

Bible Verse:

What stands out to you?	Spirit & Soul. Action Plan
How can you apply this to your life today?	Mind. Restore & Grounding

Wellness Activity	Food Intake

Reflection & Prayer

SPIRITUAL WELLNESS EXERCISE (SWE): DAY 64

Date: _____

Bible Verse:

What stands out to you?	Spirit & Soul. Action Plan
How can you apply this to your life today?	Mind. Restore & Grounding

Wellness Activity	Food Intake

Reflection & Prayer

SPIRITUAL WELLNESS EXERCISE (SWE): DAY 65

Date: _____

Bible Verse:

What stands out to you?	Spirit & Soul. Action Plan
How can you apply this to your life today?	Mind. Restore & Grounding

Wellness Activity	Food Intake

Reflection & Prayer

SPIRITUAL WELLNESS EXERCISE (SWE): DAY 66

Date: _____

Bible Verse:

What stands out to you?	**Spirit & Soul. Action Plan**
How can you apply this to your life today?	**Mind. Restore & Grounding**

Wellness Activity	Food Intake

Reflection & Prayer

SPIRITUAL WELLNESS EXERCISE (SWE): DAY 67

Date: _____

Bible Verse:

What stands out to you?	Spirit & Soul. Action Plan
How can you apply this to your life today?	Mind. Restore & Grounding

Wellness Activity	Food Intake

Reflection & Prayer

SPIRITUAL WELLNESS EXERCISE (SWE): DAY 68

Date: _____

Bible Verse:

What stands out to you? How can you apply this to your life today?	Spirit & Soul. Action Plan Mind. Restore & Grounding

Wellness Activity	Food Intake

Reflection & Prayer

SPIRITUAL WELLNESS EXERCISE (SWE): DAY 69

Date: _____

Bible Verse:

What stands out to you?	**Spirit & Soul. Action Plan**
How can you apply this to your life today?	**Mind. Restore & Grounding**

Wellness Activity	Food Intake

Reflection & Prayer

SPIRITUAL WELLNESS EXERCISE (SWE): DAY 70

Date: _____

Bible Verse:

What stands out to you?	Spirit & Soul. Action Plan
How can you apply this to your life today?	Mind. Restore & Grounding

Wellness Activity	Food Intake

Reflection & Prayer

MOTIVATIONAL MESSAGE #4

Surrender to God's plan.

MOTIVATION & PRAYER

Focus: Gratitude & Purpose

Reflect on a prayer you've written that you feel most connected to.

Prompts:

- *This prayer resonates with me because . . .*
- *My accomplishments include . . .*
- *In my spirit, I felt . . . while achieving these goals.*

Purpose: Celebrate progress, acknowledge God's role in your journey, and renew motivation for the final stretch.

My prayer: Lord, thank You for forgiving my sins and for healing me. Thank You for the understanding, knowledge, and spirit You have placed in me to glorify You. I am grateful for a dedicated spirit to guide me in fulfilling Your purpose. I accept Your healing and thank You for renewing my mind through Your sacrifice on the cross. Thank You for filling me with peace, joy, victory, and motivation to serve You and others. I claim all the blessings You have prepared for me in the present and future. Amen.

This prayer is one I have said many times because it reflects my current sense of forgiveness and renewed self. Being connected to God each day has opened my eyes to the opportunities He wants me to pursue. For example, while on a walk recently, I realized I have the chance to support youth and help them know Christ in an interactive way. I also realized this journal could serve as a resource to bring hope to those incarcerated—something I had never considered before. In thinking about supporting those incarcerated, a thought occurred about my dad and I wondered how a resource like this could have impacted him.

Reflection Activity

- Share the prayer you feel most connected to and why.
- List some of the tasks you have accomplished over the past seventy days in your Spirit/Soul Action Plan.
- Reflect on how these accomplishments made you feel.

Prayer	Spirit & Soul. Action Plan

This prayer resonates with me because _____

_____

_____

My accomplishments include _____

_____

_____

_____

What was the feeling you had in your spirit and soul as you were accomplishing the goals?

_____

For me, as I began achieving my goals consistently, I felt in my spirit that God was guiding me every step of the way to ensure my success. One of my goals was to start a business, and I give God all the praise for this. I have launched my business, am in the process of creating the website, and opportunities are already arising that allow me to pursue my dreams while fulfilling my purpose.

Here are some sample prayers that you can use and build upon throughout days 71–90.

Commitment

Lord, thank You for giving me direction and strength. I put on the body armor of God to stay protected and led by the Holy Spirit. I trust your timing, even when it's delayed or unclear. Thank You for giving me a committed spirit and mindset. I trust You fully to do what You said You would do. Amen.

Activation

Thank You, Lord, for activating me so that my actions align with my prayers. Lead me in Your direction and help me stay focused. I have dominion through prayer, and I declare victory over every challenge before me. Amen.

Faith

Lord, thank You for giving me faith that leaves behind old ways of thinking. My faith gives me new capacity, courage, and strength. I will not settle, fear, or be limited by my past. Through faith, I claim victory and walk in righteousness. Amen.

Challenges

Lord, thank You for every challenge that expands my capacity. I trust You in trials and will not run from them. With Your grace, I have the confidence to handle anything before me. Amen.

Family

Lord, thank You for restoring my family. What once was broken is now healing through You. Thank You for sparking change in me so I can lead my family back to You. Protect us, bless us, and keep us connected to You. Amen.

AUTHOR EXAMPLE #3

(Use this content on the next page to create Example #2.)

SPIRITUAL WELLNESS EXERCISE (SWE)

Bible Verse: Luke 14:25-27

What stands out to you?

What stands out is that there is a reason why I am going through this process, as it is for a bigger cause than I can even imagine. I have my wonderings about the kind of impact it can have, and I believe that is when faith steps in to just trust what God is calling you to do.

How can you apply this to your life today?

For me, today, I am going to embrace being uncomfortable and step out of my comfort zone. I feel this message was shared with me as I am stepping out of my comfort zone with many things that have been transpiring. Creating this journal was out of my comfort zone. I understood the impact it was having on my life, and to be able to share it has been, a lot of times, scary because of the fear of the unknown and what others will say when it is published.

Spirit & Soul. Action Plan

- I am going to present to admin a new procedure for meeting with parents.
- I am going to add fifteen more seconds to each isometric exercise.
- I am going to sign up for an event at church.

Mind. Restore & Grounding

- Creflo Dollar—"Overcoming Self-Deception"
- Tyrone Morrison—"Power of a Changed Attitude (Moving from Blindness to Vision)"
- Many aha moments. When connected, we have a clear vision of things that are around us, and God can help when we may be falling into a trap of self-deception. In addition, when you are in clear vision through God, you know your purpose, and when you know your purpose, your mind is renewed. You have the strength to go out and accomplish the things that God wants you to do.

Wellness Activity

I did a lower body workout that consisted of doing a lot of isometric exercises.

Food Intake

- Coffee
- Yogurt
- Protein shake
- Rice and Chicken
- Toast

Reflection & Prayer

Thank you, Lord for providing me with opportunities to step out of my comfort zone. I ask that You continue to show me ways in which I can grow in my faith as I fulfill the purpose that you have instilled in me. Amen.

Spiritual Wellness Exercises:
Days 71–80

SPIRITUAL WELLNESS EXERCISE (SWE): DAY 71

Date: _____

Bible Verse:

What stands out to you?	Spirit & Soul. Action Plan
How can you apply this to your life today?	Mind. Restore & Grounding

Wellness Activity	Food Intake

Reflection & Prayer

SPIRITUAL WELLNESS EXERCISE (SWE): DAY 72

Date: _____

Bible Verse:

What stands out to you? How can you apply this to your life today?	Spirit & Soul. Action Plan Mind. Restore & Grounding

Wellness Activity	Food Intake

Reflection & Prayer

SPIRITUAL WELLNESS EXERCISE (SWE): DAY 73

Date: _____

Bible Verse:

What stands out to you?

Spirit & Soul. Action Plan

How can you apply this
to your life today?

Mind. Restore & Grounding

Wellness Activity

Food Intake

Reflection & Prayer

SPIRITUAL WELLNESS EXERCISE (SWE): DAY 74

Date: _____

Bible Verse:

What stands out to you?	Spirit & Soul. Action Plan
How can you apply this to your life today?	Mind. Restore & Grounding

Wellness Activity	Food Intake

Reflection & Prayer

SPIRITUAL WELLNESS EXERCISE (SWE): DAY 75

Date: _____

Bible Verse:

What stands out to you?

Spirit & Soul. Action Plan

How can you apply this
to your life today?

Mind. Restore & Grounding

Wellness Activity

Food Intake

Reflection & Prayer

SPIRITUAL WELLNESS EXERCISE (SWE): DAY 76

Date: _____

Bible Verse:

| What stands out to you?

How can you apply this to your life today? | **Spirit & Soul. Action Plan**

Mind. Restore & Grounding |

| Wellness Activity | Food Intake |

Reflection & Prayer

SPIRITUAL WELLNESS EXERCISE (SWE): DAY 77

Date: _____

Bible Verse:

What stands out to you?	Spirit & Soul. Action Plan
How can you apply this to your life today?	Mind. Restore & Grounding

Wellness Activity	Food Intake

Reflection & Prayer

SPIRITUAL WELLNESS EXERCISE (SWE): DAY 78

Date: _____

Bible Verse:

What stands out to you? How can you apply this to your life today?	Spirit & Soul. Action Plan Mind. Restore & Grounding

Wellness Activity	Food Intake

Reflection & Prayer

SPIRITUAL WELLNESS EXERCISE (SWE): DAY 79

Date: _____

Bible Verse:

What stands out to you?	Spirit & Soul. Action Plan
How can you apply this to your life today?	Mind. Restore & Grounding

Wellness Activity	Food Intake

Reflection & Prayer

SPIRITUAL WELLNESS EXERCISE (SWE): DAY 80

Date: _____

Bible Verse:

What stands out to you? How can you apply this to your life today?	Spirit & Soul. Action Plan Mind. Restore & Grounding

Wellness Activity	Food Intake

Reflection & Prayer

MOTIVATIONAL MESSAGE #5

Rest your mind as your time and season will come with patience.

Spiritual Wellness Exercises:
Days 81–90

SPIRITUAL WELLNESS EXERCISE (SWE): DAY 81

Date: _____

Bible Verse:

What stands out to you?	Spirit & Soul. Action Plan
How can you apply this to your life today?	Mind. Restore & Grounding

Wellness Activity	Food Intake

Reflection & Prayer

SPIRITUAL WELLNESS EXERCISE (SWE): DAY 82

Date: _____

Bible Verse:

What stands out to you?	Spirit & Soul. Action Plan
How can you apply this to your life today?	Mind. Restore & Grounding

Wellness Activity	Food Intake

Reflection & Prayer

SPIRITUAL WELLNESS EXERCISE (SWE): DAY 83

Date: _____

Bible Verse:

What stands out to you?

Spirit & Soul. Action Plan

How can you apply this
to your life today?

Mind. Restore & Grounding

Wellness Activity

Food Intake

Reflection & Prayer

SPIRITUAL WELLNESS EXERCISE (SWE): DAY 84

Date: _____

Bible Verse:

What stands out to you?	Spirit & Soul. Action Plan
How can you apply this to your life today?	Mind. Restore & Grounding

Wellness Activity	Food Intake

Reflection & Prayer

SPIRITUAL WELLNESS EXERCISE (SWE): DAY 85

Date: _____

Bible Verse:

What stands out to you?	Spirit & Soul. Action Plan
How can you apply this to your life today?	Mind. Restore & Grounding

Wellness Activity	Food Intake

Reflection & Prayer

SPIRITUAL WELLNESS EXERCISE (SWE): DAY 86

Date: _____

Bible Verse:

What stands out to you?	Spirit & Soul. Action Plan
How can you apply this to your life today?	Mind. Restore & Grounding

Wellness Activity	Food Intake

Reflection & Prayer

SPIRITUAL WELLNESS EXERCISE (SWE): DAY 87

Date: _____

Bible Verse:

What stands out to you?	Spirit & Soul. Action Plan
How can you apply this to your life today?	Mind. Restore & Grounding

Wellness Activity	Food Intake

Reflection & Prayer

SPIRITUAL WELLNESS EXERCISE (SWE): DAY 88

Date: _____

Bible Verse:

What stands out to you?	Spirit & Soul. Action Plan
How can you apply this to your life today?	Mind. Restore & Grounding

Wellness Activity	Food Intake

Reflection & Prayer

SPIRITUAL WELLNESS EXERCISE (SWE): DAY 89

Date: _____

Bible Verse:

What stands out to you?

Spirit & Soul. Action Plan

How can you apply this
to your life today?

Mind. Restore & Grounding

Wellness Activity

Food Intake

Reflection & Prayer

SPIRITUAL WELLNESS EXERCISE (SWE): DAY 90

Date: _____

Bible Verse:

What stands out to you?	Spirit & Soul. Action Plan
How can you apply this to your life today?	Mind. Restore & Grounding

Wellness Activity	Food Intake

Reflection & Prayer

Day 90—Achievement & Completion

Congratulations! You have completed the ninety-day journey! Take a moment to reflect on all the growth, breakthroughs, and lessons you've experienced during this time. For me, this journey has been transformative. I published this interactive journal and am so grateful to have shared this process with you. I am also working towards my Licensed Professional Counselor and Licensed Professional Clinical Counselor certifications. This is deeply meaningful because I know so many people struggle with mental health, and I feel called by God to use my gifts to support, serve, and make a positive impact.

Now, it's your turn. Reflect and share your experience.

Prompts for Reflection:

- What is something that happened that you didn't expect?
- I feel more connected to God by . . .
- I feel that the SWE helped me . . .
- I was able to overcome . . .
- I developed a deeper understanding of . . .
- I discovered this about me . . .
- I integrated/combined these SWE . . .
- My favorite thing about SWE . . .
- My faith in God . . .

MOTIVATIONAL MESSAGE #6

Live life with purpose.

Special Thanks

Creating and writing this interactive journal has been an incredibly rewarding experience, and I am deeply grateful for the support I've received along the way.

I want to thank the members of Miracle City Church in Minneapolis. Their warmth and encouragement were vital in guiding me back to Jesus, especially during some of my lowest moments. Thank you for never giving up on me and for always providing a place of worship and fellowship.

I also want to thank Speak the Word Church International in Golden Valley. This is the church I grew up in after moving to Minnesota from Virginia in eighth grade. Returning has been inspiring and has strengthened my family as we attend church together, growing closer in faith.

Through this journey, I have learned that God will never give up on you. He created you in His image, with a unique purpose. By seeking Him and being patient with His timing, you will gain clarity on your purpose and receive all that He has in store for you.

Thank you, and God bless!

References

Elevation Worship, "Trust in God," Radio Version Song, Oh can you imagine?, Elevation Worship Records, 2023.

Maverick City Music & Naomi Raine, "Promises," Tribl Records, 2020.

"*Pastor Randy Morrison, "Daily Habits for Conquering Life's Challenges Pt 2*," Speaktheword.org, March 9, 2025."

"*Pastor Tyrone Morrision, "The Power of a Changed Attitude Pt. 2*," Speakttheword.org, September 7, 2025."

Creflo Dollar, "*Renewing the Mind God's Way*," Creflodollarministires.org, March 8, 2020.

Creflo Dollar, "*Overcoming Self-Deception*," Creflodollarministries.org, August 15, 2025.

Marvin Sapp, "*Here I Am (Deluxe Version)*," Verify Gospel Music Group, a unit of Sony Music Entertainment, 2010.

Zondervan, *Holy Bible: New International Version*, Zondervan, 2011, https://www.biblegateway.com.